THE ULTIMATE GUIDE TO AN ECONOMICAL LIVING

Budget Wisely, Plan Ahead, Clear Debts, and Embrace a Fulfilling Lifestyle

BY

AMBER G. SALLEE

TABLE OF CONTENTS

INTRODUCTION

Embark on a transformative journey to financial empowerment with "The Ultimate Guide to an Economical Living" by Amber G. Sallee. In this comprehensive guidebook, Amber, a devoted mother, accomplished businesswoman, and seasoned economist, invites readers to discover the keys to a more financially conscious and fulfilling life. Rooted in practical wisdom, this book transcends traditional financial advice, offering a unique blend of relatable anecdotes, savvy economic insights, and actionable strategies.

Through her lens, she explores the concept of economical living, demonstrating that with the right mindset and practical guidance, anyone can achieve financial well-being. Amber's expertise as a businesswoman adds a layer of real-world applicability to her teachings, making her advice resonate with those navigating the complexities of personal and professional life.

"The Ultimate Guide to an Economical Living" is not just a manual on managing money; it's a roadmap to a holistic, economically conscious lifestyle. Each chapter delves into practical strategies, insightful stories, and actionable steps, ensuring that readers can seamlessly integrate economic principles into their daily routines. From budgeting basics to thrifty culinary adventures, Amber's guidebook covers a spectrum of topics with simplicity and depth, offering a valuable resource for readers worldwide.

In a world where financial literacy is paramount, Amber G. Sallee's book stands as a beacon, guiding readers towards financial freedom and a more purposeful life. Whether you're a parent, an aspiring entrepreneur, or someone seeking to enhance your economic resilience, this guide provides the tools to reshape your financial narrative. Join Amber on this empowering journey, and let "The Ultimate Guide to an Economical Living" be your companion in building a brighter financial future.

CHAPTER 1

EMBRACING ECONOMICAL LIVING - A PRACTICAL GUIDE TO DEFINE ECONOMIC LIVING

Welcome to the practical world of Economic Living—a lifestyle that goes beyond budgeting and embraces a mindset of intentional choices and resource optimization. In this chapter, we'll delve into the essence of economic living, breaking it down into relatable concepts and offering real-world insights to guide you on this transformative journey.

UNDERSTANDING ECONOMIC LIVING

At its core, economic living is about making your money work for you in the most efficient and purposeful way possible. It's a holistic approach that considers not just the financial aspect but also your values, goals, and overall well-being.

1. Conscious Spending: Economic living starts with a conscious approach to spending. It's about asking you, "Does this purchase align with my values and priorities?" By being mindful of your spending, you begin to see money not just as currency but as a tool to build the life you desire.

2. Prioritizing Essentials: Identify your true needs versus wants. Focus on the essentials—housing, utilities, quality food—while being discerning about non-essential purchases. This doesn't mean cutting out enjoyment but ensuring your spending reflects your priorities.

3. Smart Debt Management: Economic living involves using debt judiciously. Avoid accumulating unnecessary debt, especially for non-essential items. Prioritize paying off high-interest debts and consider debt only when it aligns with long-term goals.

4. Quality over Quantity: Invest in quality items that provide long-term value. While this might mean a higher initial cost, it often pays off in the long run. Economic living encourages a shift from a disposable mindset to one of durability and value.

5. Embracing a DIY Mentality: Cultivate a do-it-yourself mindset where feasible. Learning basic skills for home repairs, maintenance, or even cooking not only saves money but also fosters a sense of empowerment and self-sufficiency.

6. Resourcefulness in Action: Practice resourcefulness by exploring alternatives before making a purchase. Whether it's finding budget-friendly options or repurposing items, being resourceful opens up creative solutions to everyday challenges.

7. Continuous Learning and Adaptation: Economic living is not a static concept; it evolves with your life. Stay informed about personal finance, budgeting strategies, and new opportunities. Continuous learning empowers you to adapt your financial approach as circumstances change.

CONSCIOUS GROCERY SHOPPING

Emma, a working professional, noticed her grocery bills were escalating. She decided to apply economic living principles to her grocery shopping.

- **Create a Meal Plan:** Plan your meals for the week, taking inventory of what you already have.
- **Shopping List:** Based on your meal plan, create a detailed shopping list to avoid impulsive purchases.

- **Buy in Bulk:** Purchase non-perishable items in bulk to save on unit costs.
- **Explore Discounts:** Take advantage of discounts, loyalty programs, and coupons to maximize savings.
- **Compare Prices:** Compare prices across different brands and stores to ensure you're getting the best value for your money.

QUALITY OVER QUANTITY IN CLOTHING

James found himself with a wardrobe full of clothes, many of which he rarely wore. He decided to adopt an economic approach to his clothing choices.

- **Capsule Wardrobe:** Streamline your wardrobe with a capsule collection of versatile, high-quality pieces.
- **Invest in Timeless Pieces:** Instead of frequent, low-quality purchases, invest in timeless, durable items that withstand trends.
- **Second-Hand Shopping:** Explore thrift stores or online platforms for gently-used clothing at a fraction of the cost.
- **Maintenance Matters:** Learn basic clothing maintenance to extend the lifespan of your

garments, reducing the need for frequent replacements.

DIY HOME SOLUTIONS

Sarah faced a leaky faucet and decided to channel her economic living mindset into a do-it-yourself home improvement project.

- **Online Tutorials:** Utilize online tutorials to learn basic plumbing skills.

- **Invest in Quality Tools:** Purchase quality tools for home maintenance, ensuring long-term usability.

- **DIY Repairs:** Attempt the faucet repairs independently, applying the skills learned.

- **Budget-Friendly Materials:** Opt for budget-friendly, durable materials for repairs.

MINDFUL ENTERTAINMENT SPENDING

John realized he was spending a significant portion of his income on entertainment. He sought to economize without sacrificing enjoyment.

- **Budget Allocation:** Allocate a specific budget for entertainment to avoid overspending.
- **Explore Free Options:** Seek out free or low-cost entertainment alternatives in your community.
- **Subscription Audits:** Evaluate subscription services; unsubscribe from those you underutilize.
- **Plan Social Activities:** Plan social activities that align with your budget, such as picnics or game nights.

By incorporating these examples and actionable steps into your daily routine, economic living becomes not just a concept but a tangible and sustainable lifestyle. As we continue this exploration, envision how these principles can be applied to various aspects of your life, transforming the way you manage and allocate your resources.

UNPACKING THE ESSENCE OF ECONOMIC LIVING - A HUMAN-CENTRIC EXPLORATION

Economic living is more than just a set of financial principles; it's a lifestyle that shapes the way we view and interact with the resources available to us. Let's delve into the core of economic living, using relatable examples and personal reflections to bring this concept to life.

THE HEART OF ECONOMIC LIVING

1. Conscious Decision-Making: Economic living, for me, begins with intentional decision-making. It's about pausing before each financial choice and asking, "Does this align with my values and contribute positively to my life?" This mindset shift has transformed how I approach everything from daily purchases to long-term investments.

2. Prioritizing Needs over Wants: I vividly recall a moment when I decided to prioritize needs over wants. Instead of succumbing to impulse purchases, I began evaluating whether an item brought genuine value to my life. This shift not only curbed unnecessary spending but also brought a sense of purpose to every purchase.

3. Quality Investments: In the realm of economic living, I've come to appreciate the value of quality over quantity. It's not about accumulating possessions but investing in items that withstand the test of time. My decision to invest in a durable, albeit slightly pricier, backpack proved to be a game-changer—it outlasted multiple cheaper alternatives.

4. Crafting a Budget with Purpose: Budgeting took on a new meaning when I approached it with purpose. Rather than viewing it as a restrictive tool, I saw it as a guide to align my spending with my goals. I created categories not just for bills but for experiences and personal growth, making my budget a reflection of my aspirations.

5. The Power of Saying "No": Saying "no" became a powerful tool in my economic living toolkit. I learned to decline invitations or purchases that didn't resonate with my financial goals. It's not about deprivation; it's about consciously choosing where my resources go to maximize joy and fulfillment.

6. DIY Mindset in Action: One Saturday, faced with a leaky faucet, I decided to embrace the DIY mindset. Armed with online tutorials and a basic toolkit, I successfully fixed the issue. The sense of accomplishment and the money saved reinforced the idea that learning practical skills enhances my ability to live economically.

7. Cleverness and Imagination: Living on a budget fosters creativity. Instead of going to the mall when I needed to update my wardrobe, I went to thrift stores. This set aside cash as well as presented an innovative component — I uncovered extraordinary pieces that mirrored my style all the more really.

8. Practical Decisions: Living financially is additionally about going with supportable decisions. I started using practices like composting and turned my attention to eco-friendly products. It's a little commitment to a bigger ecological effect, lining up with the more extensive ethos of monetary living.

The journey of self-discovery and intentional living is the essence of economic living. There's no need to focus on embracing an inflexible arrangement of rules, however , about understanding the significant effect every choice has on my life and my general surroundings.

Through these models, I've discovered that financial living is a dynamic and profoundly private experience, forming the story of my life in significant ways. As we proceed with this investigation, how about we uncover more features of financial living that resound with our singular stories.

EMBARKING ON THE ADVENTURE OF RESOURCE ALLOCATION WITH SMARTNESS: AN IN-DEPTH LOOK AT MY LIFE'S EXPERIENCES AND LESSONS

The process of developing a mindset that is focused on smart resource allocation has been a rich tapestry of experiences, each of which has taught me valuable lessons. How about we dive further into these encounters, disentangling the complexities of examples advanced en route.

1. Careful Utilization: The acknowledgment that my streaming memberships were discreetly siphoning away assets without adding critical worth was a vital second. It showed me the significance of careful utilization. By rethinking and dropping pointless memberships, I set aside cash as well as cleaned up my advanced space and, therefore, my psychological space.

2. Planning with Reason: Changing planning from an unremarkable undertaking into a reason driven practice was a unique advantage. I started to assign reserves to bills as well as to encounters that advanced my life. A weekend escape or putting resources into a course became costs as well as interests in my self-improvement and prosperity.

3. Key Speculations: Sarah's essential interest in a quality bike exhibited the craft of reasoning long haul. Past the prompt expense, she considered in the possible reserve funds on transportation and the medical advantages of cycling. I gained insight into the significance of strategic investments that are in line with both short-term and long-term objectives from this experience.

4. Better standards without compromise: The long-term significance of choosing quality over quantity was demonstrated by Alex's decision to prioritize a high-quality laptop over the accumulation of multiple gadgets. It re-imagined my way to deal with buys, accentuating the drawn out advantages and fulfillment got from strong and significant belongings.

5. Learning the Craft of Discussion: Seeing Sarah haggle with project workers during a home remodel wasn't simply an illustration in setting aside cash; it was schooling in strengthening. The acknowledgment that discussion isn't about a showdown however about declaring one's necessities and finding a commonly helpful arrangement turned into a foundation in my asset distribution reasoning.

6. Resilience in the Real World: The extraordinary force of genius unfurled when I chose to reuse and upcycle existing furnishings. This involved experience set aside cash as well as started a feeling of inventiveness and fulfillment. It was a lesson about how, if we approach challenges with an open mind, solutions are frequently found in our immediate surroundings.

7. Putting money into skill development: Imprint's excursion of putting resources into coding abilities enlightened the more extensive range of asset portion. It exhibited that ventures aren't restricted to financial exchanges however stretch out to self-improvement. Ability obtaining, I understood, is a speculation that delivers profits all through one's life.

8.   Eco-Accommodating   Living: Emma's obligation to eco-accommodating living wasn't simply a natural decision; it was a monetary methodology with a soul. Reusable products' initial price became an investment in sustainability, resulting in lower long-term costs and a greener, more responsible lifestyle.

9. Local area coordinated effort: Sorting out and taking part in local area trade occasions woke me up to the force of cooperative asset portion. It changed the manner in which I saw local area commitment, understanding that sharing assets inside the area decreased individual spending as well as cultivated a feeling of public obligation.

10. Vital using time effectively: Time, frequently ignored as an asset, arose as a significant part of brilliant asset designation. Vital using time effectively, focusing on undertakings lined up with my objectives, turned into a significant illustration. There wasn't really any need to focus on doing all the more however about improving time for what genuinely made a difference.

Through these encounters and the related illustrations, I've come to comprehend that savvy asset allotment rises above monetary choices. An outlook pervades each feature of life, directing decisions that line up with individual qualities, long haul objectives, and the prosperity of the two people and networks. The excursion proceeds, with each experience adding one more layer to the developing account of living insightfully and purposefully. Go along with me in this odyssey where astuteness is gathered from the regular embroidery of life's examples.

EMBARKING ON THE JOURNEY TO ECONOMICAL BLISS: STEPS FOR A HAPPIER, MORE THRIFTY LIFE

Alright, let's break down how to dive into this whole economical living thing. It's not just about saving money; it's about finding joy in being savvy with your resources. Let's keep it real and relatable.

1. Live below Your Means: Start by checking in with your lifestyle. Are there areas where you can cut back without feeling like you're sacrificing your happiness? It's not about pinching pennies; it's about making intentional choices that leave you feeling good. So, I looked at my subscriptions and realized I was paying for stuff I hardly used. Cancelled a few, and suddenly, I had extra cash for things I actually enjoyed.

2. Try the Quick-Start Spending Freeze: Ever heard of a spending freeze? It's like pressing pause on non-essential spending for a bit. Take a look at where your money usually goes and hit the pause button on things that aren't bringing you real joy right now. I declared a "No-Spend Weekend." Skipped the impulse buys and ended up saving more than I thought.

3. Begin Your Spending Freeze Journey: It's not just about freezing spending; it's about understanding why you spend. Take a moment before each purchase and ask, "Do I really need this, or am I just bored?" Small changes lead to big results. I started questioning my purchases. Turns out, half the stuff I was buying was just to kill time. Now, I buy things I genuinely love.

4. Give Yourself a Spending Allowance: No one likes feeling deprived. Set aside a chunk of your budget for guilt-free spending. It's your personal allowance to splurge a bit without wrecking your budget. I call it my "Fun Fund." Having a set amount to spend on whatever I want makes sticking to my budget way less stressful.

5. Sort Out Essential Bills First: Make sure your essential bills are sorted. Automate payments if you can, so you can focus on enjoying life without worrying about overdue bills. I automated my bills, and suddenly, I had more mental space to think about things I enjoy rather than due dates.

6. Stop Being a Mindless Customer: Ever catch yourself buying stuff just because it's on sale or looks cool? Switch off that autopilot "customer" mode. Pause before purchases and ask, "Do I really need this, or am I falling for a marketing trick?" I started waiting 24 hours before buying anything non-essential. Most times, I realized I didn't need it that badly.

7. Check Your Stamina for This Lifestyle: Living economically is a marathon, not a sprint. Check in with yourself regularly. What's working? What's tough? Celebrate the wins and adjust your game plan as needed. Every few months, I look at what's been easy and what's been challenging. It keeps me on track without feeling like I'm on a strict budget.

8. Make Frugality Your Friend: Frugality isn't about being cheap; it's about being smart with your money.

See it as a tool to fund your dreams, not a punishment. Instead of thinking, "I can't afford this," I started asking, "How can I afford this?" It's a game-changer.

9. Go Green and Save: Think beyond your wallet; consider the planet too. Small changes like using reusable stuff not only save money in the long run but also reduce waste. I switched to reusable shopping bags and water bottles. It felt good saving money and doing a tiny bit for the environment.

10. Learn a Bit about Money: Financial literacy isn't just for finance nerds. Knowing the basics helps you make smarter choices. Take some time to learn—it's an investment in yourself. I started with some YouTube videos and easy-to-read books. Now I understand my money way better, and it's less intimidating.

So there you have it—practical steps, real-life examples, and a bit of humor to make this whole economical living thing a joyous journey. It's not about deprivation; it's about making choices that bring you happiness without breaking the bank. Enjoy the ride! 🚀

CHAPTER 2

FINANCIAL AWARENESS: MONEY MATTERS TALK

Alright, let's have a good old-fashioned chat about money because, let's face it, it's a big part of our lives. No need for fancy jargon or complicated terms - just some real talk about financial awareness and why it matters.

THE BASICS - MONEY IS MORE THAN JUST BILLS

So, money, right? It's not just about paying bills and avoiding debt. It's about having the freedom to do the things you love, whether that's traveling, enjoying a good meal, or just having a stress-free weekend. Last month, I splurged a bit on a weekend getaway. It felt so good knowing I had the financial freedom to treat myself without stressing about the budget.

FACING THE FEAR - UNDERSTANDING YOUR FINANCES

Okay, let's address the elephant in the room—many of us avoid looking at our bank statements like it's a horror movie. But guess what? Understanding your finances is like knowing the plot twist before it happens. It's empowering. I used to be terrified of checking my bank balance. Now, it's like facing a fear; once you do it, it's not that bad, and you feel more in control.

SAVING FOR WHAT MATTERS - IT'S NOT JUST ABOUT THE EMERGENCY FUND

Sure, we've all heard about having an emergency fund, but let's talk beyond that. Saving is like planting seeds for your future goals. Whether it's a dream vacation, a house, or just some peace of mind, it all starts with saving. I started a "Dream Fund" for that epic road trip I've always wanted to take. Even putting in a small amount each month feels like I'm investing in my own happiness.

DEBT DEMONS - TAMING THE CREDIT CARD MONSTER

Credit cards—they can be a blessing or a curse. It's all about taming the plastic beast. Paying off those balances and using credit wisely is like taking control of your financial narrative. I once had a credit card balance that felt like a monster haunting me. Slowly but surely, I chipped away at it. The relief when it hit zero was indescribable.

BUDGETING - IT'S NOT A STRAITJACKET, IT'S A PLAN

Budgeting—it sounds restrictive, but think of it as your financial GPS. It's not about saying "no" to everything; it's about saying "yes" to the things that matter most. It's your roadmap to financial success. I thought budgeting meant no more fun. Turns out, it just helped me prioritize. I still have fun, but now I know where my money is going.

INVESTING - YOUR MONEY CAN WORK FOR YOU

Investing—it's not just for Wall Street big shots. Putting your money to work in the right places can grow it over time. It's like having little money minions out there making more money for you. I started investing a small amount regularly. It's not about being a stock market genius; it's about giving your money a chance to grow over time.

LEARNING AND GROWING - FINANCIAL LITERACY MATTERS

Think of financial literacy as the cheat codes to the money game. The more you understand, the better you play. It's not about being a financial wizard; it's about making informed decisions. I used to feel lost when people talked about interest rates and investments. Now, a bit of YouTube and some easy reads later, and I feel way more in the know.

COMMUNITY VIBES - MONEY TALK WITH FRIENDS

Money can be a taboo topic, but let's break that barrier. Talking about money with friends can bring new perspectives, ideas, and even some laughs. We're all on this financial journey together. I started having "money dates" with a friend. We share tips, victories, and even our money mishaps. It's like a support group, but for your wallet.

FINAL THOUGHTS - MONEY IS A TOOL, NOT THE END GAME

In the grand scheme of things, money is a tool to help you live the life you want. It's not the end goal; it's the means to create memorable experiences, pursue passions, and build a future that brings you joy. I used to stress about money all the time. Now, I see it as a tool that I control, not the other way around. It's freeing.

So there you have it—a good money matters talk. No suits, no ties, just some honest thoughts about navigating the financial maze. Money is a part of life, so let's make it a conversation, not a mystery. Cheers to financial awareness!

UNRAVELING THE LAYERS OF ECONOMIZING ESSENTIALS WITH RICH NARRATIVES AND PROFOUND INSIGHTS - UNVEILING THE TRUE ESSENTIALS

The supermarket, a modern-day labyrinth of choices. As I strolled down the aisles with Sarah, she shared her transformational journey from impulsive buying to intentional shopping. Sarah's list wasn't just about groceries; it was a curated selection of needs and conscious indulgences. Each item had a purpose, a nutritional value, and a designated place in her weekly menu. It wasn't merely economizing; it was a culinary strategy designed for both the health of her body and her budget.

REDEFINING NECESSITIES

Tom's realization about the gym was a paradigm shift. It wasn't just about economizing but about crafting a lifestyle that aligned with his values. Home workouts weren't just a budget-friendly alternative; they became a celebration of simplicity. The whirring treadmill was replaced by the fresh air of his backyard, and the clanking of weights gave way to the serenity of self-paced exercises. It was more than economizing; it was finding joy in the essentials.

IDENTIFYING AND PRIORITIZING TRUE NECESSITIES

In the midst of Marie Kondo-ing her closet, Maria uncovered a profound truth about the emotional baggage tied to material possessions. Her minimalist journey wasn't merely about economizing space but about creating a mental sanctuary. Each piece she retained told a story, brought her joy, and contributed to a curated collection that resonated with her true self. Economizing wasn't just about budgeting; it was about decluttering the soul.

STREAMLINING THE MONTHLY BILLS

John's journey through bill negotiation wasn't a mundane financial task; it was a declaration of financial independence. His phone calls to service providers were strategic moves in a chess game of personal finance. Each negotiated rate wasn't just a reduction in expenses; it was a victory, a reclaiming of control over his financial narrative. Economizing, in this context, became a form of empowerment.

CURBING IMPULSE BUYS

Emily's "book wish list" wasn't a mere tactic to cut down on book expenses; it was a shift in mindset. Each book on the list was a carefully chosen companion, not a fleeting fancy. The delayed gratification transformed the act of purchasing into a deliberate and cherished decision. It was economizing not just money but investing in a curated literary journey.

DISTINGUISHING BETWEEN WANTS AND NEEDS

Alex's introduction of a "cooling-off" period before gadget purchases was more than a financial strategy; it was a lesson in self-awareness. It wasn't just about economizing on gadgets; it was a practice in distinguishing between momentary desires and genuine needs. The waiting period allowed him to assess the true necessity of each purchase, unveiling the essence of economizing beyond the financial realm.

MEAL PLANNING FOR ECONOMIC WINS

Chloe's joy in meal planning was a revelation in culinary economizing. It wasn't just about saving money on groceries; it was a creative exploration of flavors and a conscious effort to minimize food wastage. Each planned meal wasn't a mere item on a budget; it was a culinary masterpiece, a canvas painted with economic and gastronomic prowess.

BARGAIN HUNTING AND THRIFT SHOPPING

Brian's love for vintage furniture became a lesson in economic aesthetics. Thrifting wasn't just about saving money; it was a treasure hunt, a curated collection of pieces with character and history. Each thrifted find wasn't a compromise but a statement—a testament to the marriage of economic prudence and unique style.

DOWNSCALING FOR ECONOMIC COMFORT

Lisa's decision to downsize her apartment wasn't just a logistical move; it was a philosophical shift. It wasn't just about economizing space; it was about embracing a minimalist lifestyle. Each piece of furniture in her smaller abode wasn't just functional; it was a deliberate choice, a statement on the beauty of simplicity. Economizing wasn't a limitation but a liberation.

TECH DETOX FOR FINANCIAL WELLNESS

Mike's tech detox wasn't a mere hiatus from gadgets; it was a recalibration of priorities. It wasn't just about economizing on tech expenses; it was a journey of appreciating the functionality of existing devices. Each moment away from the constant upgrades became a revelation—a realization that economizing wasn't just about gadgets but about reclaiming time, attention, and mental space.

Economizing the essentials, when examined at its core, isn't a mere exercise in frugality. It's a profound exploration of values, priorities, and intentional living. It's about creating a lifestyle that resonates with our true selves, where each economizing decision is a conscious step towards a life rich in experiences, meaning, and financial freedom. 🌿☀

LUXURIES REIMAGINED: NAVIGATING THE DEPTHS OF CONSCIOUS LIVING

Luxuries, those alluring facets of life, often entwine with our identity and societal norms. To truly grasp the essence of reimagining luxuries, we must plunge into the depths of personal experiences, dissect transformative moments, and explore the intricacies of this profound journey.

The realization of drowning in excess was not a mere acknowledgment of cluttered spaces; it was an awakening to the burden of material possessions on my mental and emotional well-being. Amanda's odyssey into minimalism mirrored this sentiment, as her closet metamorphosis symbolized shedding layers of superficiality, leaving behind only the essence of her true self.

Living with fewer possessions wasn't a constrained existence; it was a canvas where limitations birthed creativity. This transformative experiment extended beyond a temporary challenge; it marked a paradigm shift in my relationship with materialism. Jake's digital detox, too, wasn't a momentary pause. It was a deliberate choice to infuse intentionality into every digital interaction, uncovering a wealth of meaningful experiences beyond the screen.

Luxuries, once confined to material opulence, took on new dimensions when redefined as experiences. This shift transcended the temporal satisfaction of possessions. Weekend getaways, moments of solitude, and genuine connections became not just luxuries but integral components of a rich and fulfilling life. Sarah's transition from spa memberships to DIY rituals underscored this metamorphosis, turning self-care into a sacred practice.

Liberation from societal expectations wasn't a solitary act; it was a courageous rebellion against the normative tide. The decision to challenge established norms and downsize life events, exemplified by Mark's intimate wedding celebration, wasn't just about economizing resources. It was an assertion of personal values over societal dictates, marking a shift from extravagance to authenticity.

Reevaluating luxuries involves more than surface-level adjustments; it demands a profound awareness of behavioral patterns and the courage to instigate change. Emily's luxury journal wasn't a mere accounting tool; it was a journey into self-discovery. The meticulous documentation of non-essential purchases empowered her to discern underlying patterns, steering her towards a path of mindful choices.

The journey into reimagining luxuries wasn't about asceticism or deprivation; it was an intentional curation of life's facets. It entailed decluttering both physical and mental spaces, fostering an environment where each possession and experience contribute meaningfully. James' embrace of digital minimalism wasn't just about simplifying his screen; it was a profound choice to clear mental clutter, allowing for a more focused and intentional life.

Reimagining luxuries isn't a linear process; it's a tapestry woven with threads of self-discovery, intentional living, and mindful choices. It's an exploration of what truly adds value to our lives. As we navigate the depths of conscious living, may this journey inspire a profound shift—a shift towards a life where luxuries, whether tangible or experiential, are chosen deliberately, each contributing to the richness of our existence.

NAVIGATING THE EMERGENCY FUND TERRAIN - A HUMAN-CENTRIC ODYSSEY

In the tumultuous seas of personal finance, there exists a steadfast lifeboat—the emergency fund. It's more than a financial cushion; it's a reliable shield against the unpredictable storms that life may hurl our way. Join me as we embark on a deep-dive exploration into the essentials of this financial safety net, grounded in real-life examples and practical wisdom, navigating the complexities with a human touch.

Consider the emergency fund as the unsung hero, ready to swoop in when life throws unexpected challenges. Sarah's car breaking down was not just a vehicular hiccup but a testament to the superhero cape her emergency fund donned. It covered the repair costs seamlessly, preventing financial chaos and showcasing the fund's fundamental role in maintaining stability. The lesson here is clear: it's not about predicting every twist and turn but acknowledging the inherent unpredictability of life and preparing accordingly.

Determining the optimal size of your emergency fund is a personalized endeavor, much like customizing a lifeboat to weather your specific financial storms. Emily's journey through sudden job loss exemplifies this. Her meticulously built emergency fund became a financial lifeboat, preventing her from drowning in debt during the turbulent seas of unemployment. This brings us to a critical realization—your financial lifeboat needs to be tailored to your unique circumstances, ensuring it can weather the storms specific to your financial landscape.

The elusive question persists: How much is enough? The three to six months' worth of living expenses guideline is a rule of thumb, but it's not one-size-fits-all. Mike's experience, navigating a delay in client payments, underscored the importance of having a financial cushion. His emergency fund, though snug, acted as a safety net until cash flow normalized. Consider the emergency fund as a financial cushion, sufficient to cover essentials if a sudden financial tempest hits.

The journey to building an emergency fund is a marathon, not a sprint. James, fresh out of college, committed to saving a portion of his income monthly. It started as a modest effort but evolved into a substantial fund that shielded him during an unforeseen medical expense. This showcases the transformative power of gradual accumulation—a financial fortress fortified over time. It's not just about the destination; it's about the journey and the resilience cultivated along the way.

Tightening your financial belt during challenging times becomes a strategic approach to emergency fund construction. Lisa, a single parent, faced unexpected home repairs. Scrutinizing her budget, cutting back on non-essential expenses, and redirecting the saved funds fortified her emergency fund. This was not a tale of deprivation but a strategic allocation of resources to build a robust financial fortress. Flexibility in budgeting and resource allocation can transform financial challenges into opportunities for fund growth.

Not every financial hiccup warrants a dip into the emergency fund. Mark's discernment, backed by clear activation criteria, prevented unnecessary depletion. Essential expenses like rent, utilities, or unforeseen medical bills made the cut. This strategic approach maintained the fund's readiness for genuine financial emergencies. Consider this as a financial triage—prioritizing the most critical needs and preserving the fund's sanctity for true emergencies.

Building an emergency fund isn't just a numbers game; it's about cultivating an emotional safety net. Chloe, a recent convert to the emergency fund lifestyle, found unexpected comfort in knowing she had a financial cushion. When her pet needed emergency medical attention, the fund not only covered vet bills but also eased the emotional strain of making swift and necessary decisions. The emotional preparedness component adds a layer of resilience, ensuring that the fund serves not only financial but also emotional needs.

Crisis-mode demands not just financial adaptability but a reassessment of emergency fund strategies. Alex, facing a sudden reduction in income, revisited his approach. He negotiated bills, explored temporary side gigs, and temporarily adjusted his lifestyle. It wasn't just about weathering the storm but actively steering through it with resilience. Crisis-oriented reassessment is the essence of financial adaptability—a key skill in maintaining the relevance and efficacy of the emergency fund.

The emergency fund is not a mere financial anchor; it's a tangible expression of preparedness in a world of uncertainties. It's a necessity, not a luxury—a lifeline that transcends financial jargon to become a practical, human-centric shield against life's unexpected challenges. As we navigate these financial waters together, may your emergency fund be sturdy, your financial journey resilient, and your peace of mind unwavering. ⚓✖

BANKROLLING YOUR EMERGENCY FUND - CRAFTING YOUR FINANCIAL SYMPHONY

Embarking on the journey to bankroll your emergency fund is akin to conducting a symphony, where each financial decision plays a crucial role in creating a harmonious melody of preparedness. Let's delve deeper into the nuances, speaking the language of real-life scenarios and practical insights.

Picture this as the beginning of a musical masterpiece—the moment you decide to allocate a portion of your income to your emergency fund. It's not just a financial move; it's a conscious decision to safeguard your financial harmony. Take John, for example. His commitment to earmark a percentage of his monthly income marked the opening notes of his financial symphony, setting the stage for preparedness.

In the symphony of financial planning, identifying areas to cut back is akin to creating distinct musical moments. Emily's story comes to mind. Facing a lean month, she scrutinized her discretionary spending. Skipping the daily latte and reducing dining out were not just sacrifices; they were impactful crescendos in her financial composition, creating a noticeable addition to her emergency fund.

Imagine this as a musical interlude—a strategic pause that introduces a new instrument. Selling underutilized assets, as Mark did with his old camera equipment, is not just a financial move. It's a deliberate choice to declutter both physical and financial spaces, creating a harmonious instrumental interlude in the bankrolling symphony.

Introduce the side hustle—a dynamic instrument that adds depth and versatility to your financial composition. Sarah's exploration of freelance writing during a period of abundance became a melodic stream of funds directed into her emergency fund. The side hustle isn't just about additional income; it's about creating a harmonious balance in your financial orchestra.

Visualize the staccato notes—a series of brief, distinct, and impactful moments. During financial tightness, embracing temporary frugality becomes the staccato of your bankrolling symphony. Alex's decision to eat inexpensively for a few weeks, redirecting the saved funds into his emergency fund, added a memorable note—a staccato of frugality—to his financial melody.

In the symphony of financial stability, minimizing fixed expenses is a harmonious adjustment—a deliberate tuning of your financial instruments. Chloe's negotiation with service providers to lower monthly bills temporarily was not just a financial decision. It was a strategic move, ensuring a harmonious crescendo of funds redirected to her emergency fund.

Envision the ensemble—the synchronized collaboration of instruments. Monthly contributions and automatic transfers play a similar role in your bankrolling symphony. James, committed to consistency, set up an automatic transfer from his checking to his emergency fund. This financial ensemble ensures a steady rhythm of contributions, forming the backbone of his financial composition.

As every symphony concludes with a coda, your journey of bankrolling your emergency fund culminates in assessing and adjusting. After a period of financial stability, Lisa reviewed her emergency fund contributions. Adjusting her monthly contribution to reflect an increase in income ensured that her financial melody remained in harmony with her evolving circumstances.

Bankrolling your emergency fund is not a solo performance but a symphony—a collaborative effort of budgeting, strategic decision-making, and financial discipline. As you navigate the complex notes of financial planning, may your emergency fund resonate as a powerful composition, creating a harmonious financial landscape that weathers the unexpected storms of life. 🎵💼

NAVIGATING FINANCIAL STORMS WITH CREATIVE FUNDING STRATEGIES FOR YOUR EMERGENCY FUND: A PERSONAL JOURNEY

Life's unpredictable twists can sometimes thrust us into financial tempests. In these storms, conventional strategies might not be enough. Let's delve deeper into creative, human-centric approaches to fund your emergency fund, transforming challenges into opportunities.

1. Rethinking Non-Essential Expenses - The Budget Makeover: Let's get real about cutting expenses—it's not just about pinching pennies but orchestrating a budget makeover. Take my friend Sarah; when her financial ship hit rough waters, she didn't just cut back on streaming services and impromptu shopping. She redefined her spending landscape, turning her budget into a lean, mean financial plan. It's about more than sacrifice; it's a strategic reshaping of your financial habits.

2. Unleashing the Power of Digital Assets - Your Virtual Treasure Trove: Your surplus possessions tell a story, and sometimes that story can be translated into virtual gold. Picture Emma, who decided to clear out her closet and host a digital garage sale. The act wasn't just about decluttering; it was like opening a treasure trove online. Her vintage finds found new homes, and the extra cash injected fresh life into her emergency fund. Your possessions can be more than clutter—they can be a virtual windfall.

3. Crafting a Side Gig - Turning Passions into Paychecks: Passion isn't just a warm fuzzy feeling; it can be a paycheck waiting to happen. Consider Jake, a tech enthusiast who turned his love for troubleshooting into a lucrative side gig. It wasn't just about the money; it was a journey into blending passion with practicality. Your hobbies could be the bridge between your love for something and an additional income stream—making financial sense and adding a dash of fulfillment.

4. The Freelancer's Playground - Navigating Gig Economy Waters: The gig economy isn't just a buzzword; it's a playground of possibilities. Susan, a graphic designer, took a plunge during a month when projects were scarce. Freelance platforms became her stage, and each project added a unique note to her symphony of income. It's about more than finding gigs; it's about creating a freelancer's narrative uniquely yours—complete with challenges, victories, and a diverse portfolio.

5. The Art of Negotiation - Lowering Fixed Expenses: Fixed expenses aren't etched in stone—they're open to negotiation. Imagine Michael, who, faced with a dip in income, picked up the phone and negotiated temporary reductions in rent and insurance premiums. It wasn't just about saving money; it was a reminder that your fixed expenses are often more flexible than you think. Negotiation is not just a financial skill; it's a tool that can carve out a path in challenging times.

6. The Savings Challenge - Transforming Thrift into Triumph: Saving money isn't always about sacrifice; it can be a thrilling challenge. Let me introduce you to Mark, who embraced a "No-Spend Challenge." The commitment wasn't just about restricting spending; it turned the act of saving into a personal triumph. Each saved dollar was a victory, and the challenge became a game of financial resilience. It's about transforming thrift into triumph, one budget-friendly decision at a time.

7. Crowdsourcing Your Safety Net - Community as a Resource: When life throws a curveball, your community can be your safety net. Emily, facing unexpected medical expenses, discovered this firsthand through a crowdfunding campaign. It's not just about financial support; it's a testament to the strength of human connections. Crowdsourcing isn't just a financial transaction; it's a bridge between individuals, showing that community is more than a network—it's a safety net woven with empathy and shared humanity.

8. The Barter System - Exchanging Skills, Building Bonds: Monetary transactions don't always define value—sometimes it's about skill exchange and building bonds. Sarah, a language tutor, engaged in a barter system, exchanging lessons for daily necessities. It wasn't just about swapping services; it was about fostering a sense of community. The barter system is a reminder that financial transactions can be more than numbers—they can be about human connections, reciprocity, and building a stronger community.

IN CONCLUSION: YOUR FINANCIAL RESILIENCE NARRATIVE

Funding your emergency fund creatively is more than a financial strategy; it's a narrative of resilience written in everyday choices. These human-centric approaches aren't just about dollars and cents—they're about crafting a story of adaptability, resourcefulness, and community. So, as you navigate the storms, remember that your emergency fund is more than a financial reservoir—it's a testament to your ability to weather the unexpected with creativity and humanity.

NAVIGATING THE NUANCES OF EMERGENCY-WORTHY EXPENSES AND RESPONSIBLE FUND UTILIZATION

Embarking on a journey to understand the intricacies of emergency-worthy expenses and responsible fund utilization requires a nuanced approach. Let's dive deeper into the various dimensions, exploring real-life scenarios and practical principles that underscore the essence of financial responsibility.

1. Unforeseen Health Emergencies - The Delicate Balance: In the realm of health emergencies, the line between urgency and necessity can be delicate. It's not just about immediate medical needs but also considering the long-term impact on your well-being.

A sudden health crisis led me to the emergency room, prompting the use of my emergency fund. Beyond immediate medical bills, it covered follow-up appointments and medications, highlighting the fund's role in sustaining my health over time.

2. Critical Home Repairs - From Immediate Fix to Long-Term Stability: Home repairs often demand swift action to prevent escalating issues. However, it's essential to view these expenses through a lens of long-term stability. Let's uncover the layers of responsible decision-making: When a burst pipe flooded my living room, the emergency fund facilitated the immediate repair. However, it also prompted a reassessment of home maintenance, leading to a strategic budget allocation for regular upkeep to prevent future emergencies.

3. Job Loss or Income Interruption - Navigating Financial Crossroads: The prospect of losing a job or experiencing income interruption brings financial uncertainty. While the emergency fund acts as a safety net, its utilization requires a strategic approach to ensure sustainable financial navigation: Job loss thrust me into uncharted territory. The emergency fund became a lifeline, covering essential expenses. Simultaneously, it initiated a reflective period, prompting a reevaluation of career choices and the pursuit of a more stable income source.

4. Vehicle Breakdowns - Beyond Immediate Fixes: A breakdown in your vehicle can disrupt daily life. While using the emergency fund for immediate repairs is justifiable, it also prompts a deeper examination of transportation-related financial planning: A significant car breakdown triggered not only the use of the emergency fund but also a comprehensive review of transportation costs. This led to the creation of a dedicated fund for routine maintenance, reducing the reliance on the emergency fund for vehicular issues.

GUIDING PRINCIPLES FOR RESPONSIBLE FUND UTILIZATION: NURTURING FINANCIAL WISDOM AT ITS CORE

As we navigate the labyrinth of responsible fund utilization, the guiding principles serve as beacons, illuminating the path to financial wisdom. Let's delve even deeper into these principles, unraveling their layers and understanding how they shape our financial choices.

1. Prioritize Essential Needs with Precision - The Art of Discernment: Prioritizing essential needs is not a blunt exercise but an art of discernment. It's about distinguishing between immediate necessities and discretionary desires, ensuring that the fund serves its purpose without compromising the quality of life.

A vivid illustration of this principle emerged when faced with a tempting offer for a luxury item. The discerning lens helped me differentiate between a genuine need and a momentary desire, reinforcing the importance of precision in prioritizing essentials.

2. Strategic Debt Management as a Financial Chess Move - Mastering the Game: Using the emergency fund to manage debt is akin to playing chess—a strategic move with long-term implications. It involves understanding the intricate dance between interest rates, financial stability, and the broader chessboard of personal finance.

Confronted with a looming mountain of high-interest credit card debt, I strategized the utilization of the emergency fund. This tactical move not only alleviated immediate financial strain but also showcased the strategic aspect of responsible fund utilization in the game of financial chess.

3. Regular Fund Replenishment - The Symphony of Financial Stability: Replenishing the emergency fund is not a mechanical task but a symphony. It involves orchestrating a harmonious interplay between income, expenses, and savings, ensuring that the fund remains a robust pillar of financial stability. After utilizing the fund for a health-related emergency, the structured monthly contribution plan became the melody of financial stability. It wasn't just about replenishing; it was about creating a financial symphony that resonated with stability and foresight.

4. Learning and Adapting - Crafting a Financial Evolution: Each utilization of the emergency fund is not just a financial transaction; it's an opportunity for learning and adaptation. It involves evolving financial strategies based on the unique lessons gleaned from every experience. Reflecting on a vehicle breakdown and the subsequent adjustment in financial strategy, I embraced the concept of financial evolution. It's not about static decisions but a dynamic process that continually adapts to the ever-changing landscape of personal finance.

In the intricate dance of responsible fund utilization, these guiding principles are not mere rules but profound philosophies that sculpt our financial journey. They are the compass, steering us through the complexities of personal finance with wisdom, discernment, and the dynamic ability to adapt.

DISCOVERING YOUR MONEY WORLD: SIMPLE REFLECTIONS FOR EVERYDAY LIVING

Exploring your money world is like taking a stroll through your thoughts about cash and spending. Let's simplify our journey by breaking down some easy prompts for thinking about money, figuring out fixed and changing expenses, and understanding how you spend your money compared to what you earn.

UNDERSTANDING YOUR MONEY WORLD - EASY QUESTIONS TO ASK YOURSELF

Question #1: "What Does Being Good with Money Mean to Me?"

Think about what being good with money looks like for you. Is it having enough for the things you enjoy or feeling secure? Understanding what matters to you is the starting point. Being good with money, for me, means having enough for things I enjoy, like going out with friends or saving for a rainy day.

Question #2: "What Money Goals Are Important to Me Right Now?"

Consider what you want to achieve with your money. Is it saving for something specific or just making sure your bills are paid on time? Right now, my goal is to save for a weekend getaway with friends. It gives me something to look forward to.

Question #3: "How Can I Deal with Money Challenges in a Simple Way?"

Think about how you handle money problems. Do you see them as opportunities to learn or just hurdles to jump over? When I faced a money challenge, I saw it as a chance to learn how to budget better. It made handling money feel less overwhelming.

Question #4: "What Gives Me Peace of Mind Regarding Money?"

Consider what brings you peace of mind when it comes to finances. Is it having a safety net for unexpected expenses or having a clear plan for your future? Peace of mind, for me, is having savings for unexpected moments and a clear plan to reach my goals.

Question #5: "How Do I Feel About Saving for the Future?"

Reflect on your emotions regarding saving. Does it feel like a burden or a source of empowerment for future possibilities? Saving for the future feels empowering; it's like planting seeds for the life I want down the road.

Question #6: "In What Ways Can I Simplify Money Management Even More?"

Think about streamlining your approach to money. Are there aspects you can simplify to make financial management less complex? I simplified my money management by setting up automatic transfers for savings. It takes away the stress of manual planning.

SORTING YOUR SPENDING - EASY WAYS TO SPLIT EXPENSES

Category #1: Fixed Expenses - Things That Stay the Same

Identify things you have to pay every month, like rent or bills. These are like the steady rocks in your spending. Rent and bills are fixed expenses. They stay the same each month.

Category #2: Variable Expenses - Things That Can Change

Look at things that might change, like how much you spend on groceries or going out. These are more flexible and can be adjusted. Groceries and dining out are variable expenses because I can decide to spend more or less on them each month.

Category #3: Recurring Subscriptions - Those Sneaky, Regular Costs

Identify recurring subscriptions that might slip under the radar. These can include streaming services, magazines, or app subscriptions. Monthly subscriptions to apps were adding up. I reconsidered and cut back on the ones I rarely used.

Category #4: Fun Treats - Budgeting for Enjoyable Moments

Look at budgeting for treats that bring joy, like a coffee from your favorite café or a small purchase that sparks happiness. I allocated a small budget for treats like a weekly coffee. It's a simple pleasure that adds joy without breaking the bank.

CHECKING YOUR SPENDING - EASY WAYS TO LOOK AT YOUR MONEY HABITS

Check #1: Creating Spending Categories - Grouping Similar Things Together

Put similar spending together, like all the money you spend on food or entertainment. It helps you see where your money is going. I grouped all my entertainment spending, and it showed me I was spending a lot on video subscriptions. I decided to cut back on some of them.

Check #2: Calculating the Percentage of Income Spent - Comparing Money In and Money Out

See how much of your money goes to each category. It gives you a simple way to understand if you're spending more than you should in certain areas. I realized I was spending a big chunk of my money on clothes. I decided to be more careful and save more instead.

Check #3: Reviewing Saving Habits - Celebrating Small Wins

Celebrate small victories in your saving habits, like constantly contributing to your emergency fund or reaching a specific savings goal. Saving consistently each month felt like a win. It showed me that small steps lead to significant financial progress.

Check #4: Reflecting on Non-Essential Spending - Balancing Enjoyment and Prudence

Balance between non-essential spending that brings joy and maintaining financial prudence. Reflect on finding that sweet spot. I realized it's okay to spend on things I enjoy as long as it aligns with my overall financial goals. It's about finding a balance.

In the simple world of thinking about money, these easy questions and categories act like a helpful guide. They make handling your money feel less like a big puzzle and more like a simple journey you can enjoy. ✳❦

NAVIGATING THE BUDGETING JOURNEY: BUILDING FINANCIAL STRENGTH

Embarking on the path of effective budgeting is like constructing a strong foundation for your financial well-being. Let's dive deeper, using simple language to explore the details of setting living expenses and creating a practical budget that fits your unique financial goals.

GRASPING YOUR FINANCIAL BASICS - SETTING THE GROUNDWORK WITH LIVING EXPENSES

Before we get into the nitty-gritty of budgeting, let's start by figuring out your money basics—establishing a baseline for living expenses, the essential costs woven into your daily life.

Fixed Expenses-The Steady Ones: Think about the bills that stay the same each month—rent or mortgage, utilities, and insurance. These are your fixed expenses, forming the stable core of your financial routine. Fixed expenses are like the dependable bills, such as rent and electricity, always with the same price. They need regular attention and financial commitment.

Variable Expenses - The Changing Components: Consider things that may vary each month—groceries, transportation, and discretionary spending. These are your variable expenses, adjusting to the unpredictable rhythm of life. Variable expenses are like groceries or social outings, changing based on life's ups and downs. Some months you might spend more, and others, you spend less.

Saving-Investing in Your Future: Amidst the regular bills, don't forget about saving. Think of it as a commitment to your future self, similar to paying a bill crucial for handling unexpected situations or achieving personal goals. Just like paying bills, I set aside some money for savings. It's like putting coins in a piggy bank for later.

CRAFTING A PRACTICAL BUDGET - TAILORING YOUR FINANCIAL PLAN

Now that we've laid the groundwork, let's move on to creating a practical budget—a flexible plan that aligns with your financial goals and lifestyle.

Analyzing Your Spending - Understanding Your Habits: Take a look at your recent spending patterns. This reflection gives valuable insights into your habits, helping you identify areas where adjustments might be helpful. Checking my recent spending showed me I was spending a bit too much on snacks. Now, I know I can cut back a little.

Categorizing Your Spending - Organizing Your Finances: Group your spending into categories—rent, food, transportation, and leisure. This structured approach makes it easier to see where your money is going, guiding sensible adjustments. Grouping expenses makes it clearer. I can see how much I spend on different parts of my life, like eating out or buying clothes.

Setting Financial Goals - Planning Your Money's Journey: Think about what you want to do with your money. Whether saving for something special or ensuring you have enough for enjoyable activities, set goals that make sense for you. My goal is to save some money each month and still have enough for things I enjoy, like going to the movies or buying a new book.

Monitoring and Adjusting - Adapting to Changes: Keep an eye on your spending compared to your budget. If you notice you're spending too much in one area, be ready to adjust your plan. Budgeting is flexible, like changing your mind when needed. I realized I spent more on clothes than I planned. So, I decided to cut back a bit and put that money into my savings goal.

Mastering budgeting isn't about using complicated words. It's like drawing a map for your money journey—a path that fits your life, ensuring your money helps you reach your goals.

CHAPTER 3

EXPLORING THE DETAILS OF PERSONAL SPENDING HABITS: A COMPREHENSIVE DIVE

To truly grasp the intricacies of individual spending habits and practical thriftiness, let's delve deeper into the strategies outlined for scrutinizing and optimizing our financial choices.

IN-DEPTH EXPLORATION OF PERSONAL SPENDING - UNVEILING SPENDING PATTERNS

a. Analyzing Spending Categories: The process of categorizing expenses goes beyond just grouping similar items—it involves a meticulous examination of each category. Consider not only where your money is going but also the value each expenditure brings to your life. As I delved into categorizing my spending, I discovered a pattern in my entertainment expenses. By scrutinizing this category, I identified areas where I could make more conscious choices and reduce unnecessary costs.

b. Setting Spending Limits: Establishing spending limits requires a nuanced understanding of your financial goals and priorities. Consider your values and allocate your resources accordingly to ensure that each category aligns with your broader financial plan. Setting a spending limit for dining out prompted me to evaluate the importance of each meal. This not only controlled my expenses but also encouraged more thoughtful choices when eating out.

c. Embracing DIY Solutions: The concept of embracing do-it-yourself solutions extends beyond mere cost-cutting. It's about fostering a sense of empowerment and self-sufficiency. Dive into learning practical skills that contribute to both savings and personal growth. Learning basic home repair skills not only saved me money on maintenance but also provided a sense of accomplishment. This shift in mindset from outsourcing to self-sufficiency transformed the way I approached various aspects of my life.

d. Regular Expense Audits: Regularly auditing expenses isn't just a financial task; it's an opportunity for self-reflection. Scrutinize each expense and question its necessity, ensuring that your financial choices align with your evolving priorities. Conducting periodic expense audits revealed subscriptions I no longer used. This exercise not only saved money but also prompted me to reassess the value each subscription added to my life.

STRATEGIES FOR FRUGAL LIVING: BEYOND COST-CUTTING

a. Prioritizing Value over Price: The principle of prioritizing value over price requires a nuanced understanding of your needs and aspirations. Consider the long-term benefits and satisfaction derived from each purchase rather than focusing solely on immediate savings. Investing in a higher-quality pair of shoes, despite the initial cost, proved to be a wise decision. The durability not only saved money over time but also enhanced my overall satisfaction with the purchase.

b. Embracing Minimalism: Embracing a minimalist lifestyle involves more than decluttering—it's a profound shift in mindset. Explore the emotional and psychological benefits of owning less and cultivating a more intentional approach to consumption. Adopting a minimalist wardrobe not only streamlined my morning routine but also significantly reduced my spending on clothing. The shift from accumulation to intentional living transformed my relationship with material possessions.

c. Smart Shopping Habits: Smart shopping isn't just about finding the best deals; it's a mindful approach to consumption. Dive into the art of discerning value, comparing prices, and making informed decisions that align with your financial goals. Strategically buying non-perishable items in bulk during sales not only saved money but also minimized the environmental impact of packaging. This dual consideration of financial and environmental implications became a cornerstone of my shopping habits.

d. Sustainable and Thrifty Choices: Consider the environmental and social impact of your purchases. Opt for sustainable choices that align with your values while contributing to a more mindful and responsible consumption pattern. Opting for up a bit of DIY was both practical and fulfilling.

e. Downsize and Declutter: Downsizing forced me to confront excess possessions. It was liberating to declutter and realize how many things I owned served no real purpose. Selling or donating them not only freed up space but also brought in extra cash.

f. Negotiate Your Bills: Initially hesitant to negotiate bills, I discovered that many service providers are open to discussions. A simple phone call helped me secure better rates, turning negotiation into a valuable skill.

UNDERSTANDING THE IMPACT OF FRUGAL CHOICES: REALIZING BROADER BENEFITS

1. Helping the Environment: Adopting eco-friendly practices within a frugal lifestyle, like reducing single-use plastics or choosing energy-efficient options, contributes to a healthier planet. This interconnectedness between personal choices and global impact is empowering.

2. Reducing Debt Faster: Witnessing the tangible effects of frugal choices on reducing debt provided a sense of financial liberation. The freedom from debt-related stress allowed for a more relaxed and confident approach to managing finances.

3. Building Long-Term Savings: The gradual accumulation of savings through frugal living isn't just about immediate financial security. It lays the foundation for future goals, whether it's homeownership, education, or early retirement.

4. Boosting Economic Resilience: The resilience gained through frugal practices became evident during economic uncertainties. Having a robust financial foundation made navigating challenges less daunting, emphasizing the significance of financial preparedness.

5. Supporting Local Communities: Recognizing the impact of choosing local businesses over large corporations highlighted the role of individual choices in community well-being. It showcased the symbiotic relationship between personal decisions and community growth.

PRACTICAL INSIGHTS AND BONUS TIPS: GOING BEYOND THE BASICS

1. Grocery Savings 101 - Scan, Plan, and Save: Utilize apps and websites that compare prices across multiple stores. This ensures you're getting the best deals without physically visiting each store. Take your planning a step further by incorporating meal prepping. It not only saves money but also time during busy weekdays.

2. DIY Home Essentials - Create, Don't Buy: Explore various online resources for eco-friendly and homemade cleaning recipes. Ingredients like lemon and essential oils can add a pleasant fragrance to your DIY cleaners. For storage solutions, consider using reusable containers instead of buying new ones. It reduces waste and saves money in the long run.

3. Subscription Audit - Trim Unnecessary Costs: Investigate your bank statements for subscriptions you might have forgotten about. Sometimes free trials turn into paid subscriptions without us realizing. If applicable, explore shared plans with family or friends for services like streaming platforms. It can significantly reduce individual costs.

4. The 24-Hour Rule - Combat Impulse Buying: Consider journaling your feelings and reasons behind wanting to make an impulse purchase. It provides deeper insights into your spending habits. Instead of buying immediately, maintain a wishlist. Revisit it after a month; you might find that some items lose their initial appeal.

5. Thrifty Transportation - Optimize Your Commute: Explore online platforms or local communities for carpooling. It not only saves money on gas but also reduces your carbon footprint. Some cities have biking initiatives with bike-sharing programs. Look into these options for a cost-effective and healthy commuting alternative.

6. Sell, Don't Hoard - Declutter for Cash: Make decluttering a seasonal activity. It's not just about selling; donating items to local charities can be fulfilling and may have tax benefits. Leverage online platforms for a virtual yard sale. It expands your reach beyond your immediate neighborhood.

7. Strategic Loyalty - Maximize Rewards: Learn the peak times for using loyalty points. Some programs offer better redemption rates during specific periods. Explore tiered memberships that offer enhanced benefits for a slightly higher fee. Assess if the added benefits align with your spending habits.

8. Energy-Efficient Habits - Trim Utility Bills: Conduct a home energy audit to identify areas of improvement. Simple changes like sealing gaps in windows can result in substantial savings. While it might require an initial investment, upgrading to energy-efficient appliances pays off over time in reduced utility bills.

9. Budget Check-In - Weekly, Not Monthly: Consider visual representations of your budget, like charts or graphs. Visuals can provide a quick overview of your financial health. Keep a diary specifically for your financial goals. Write down your aspirations and track your progress to stay motivated.

10. DIY Culinary Adventures - Cook, Freeze, and Save: Consider batching not just meals but also ingredients. For example, cook a large batch of rice or beans and freeze them in portions for quick use. Keep an inventory of your freezer. It prevents food wastage and ensures you use frozen items before they lose quality.

11. Digital Deals Mastery - Hunt for Online Discounts: Install browser extensions that automatically apply coupon codes during online checkout. It's a hassle-free way to ensure you never miss a discount. Subscribe to newsletters of your favorite stores. They often share exclusive discounts with subscribers.

12. Financial Health Check - Regular Money Physicals: Schedule detailed quarterly reviews of your financial health. Use this time to reassess your goals and make any necessary adjustments. Consider consulting a financial advisor for a comprehensive financial health check. They can provide personalized advice based on your situation.

13. The Art of Negotiation - Price Haggling: Before negotiating, thoroughly research market prices for the product or service. Knowledge is a powerful tool in negotiations. If making multiple purchases, explore the possibility of bundling them for a discounted rate. Many sellers are open to this approach.

14. Community Collaboration - Collective Savings: Join local community platforms or social media groups to stay informed about collective saving opportunities. Collaborate with your community for events like bulk purchases during sales or community-wide garage sales.

15. Rainy Day Jar - Savings in Small Coins: If you have children, involve them in the process. It becomes a fun family activity and teaches them the importance of saving. Consider creating additional jars for specific occasions, like a vacation fund or a holiday celebration fund. It adds a personalized touch to your savings strategy.

TAILORING TIPS TO DIVERSE CIRCUMSTANCES

Recognize that your financial strategies may need adjustments based on life stages. What worked as a student might need tweaking as a professional or a retiree.

CULTURAL SENSITIVITY

Be culturally sensitive in your approach. Some tips might be more applicable or resonate differently based on cultural contexts. Respect and adapt accordingly.

Remember, these tips are tools, and just like any tool, their effectiveness lies in how you use them. Tailor them to fit your unique circumstances, and view them as part of an ongoing journey toward financial well-being.

CHAPTER 4

ECONOMICAL LIVING SPACES: THRIFTY HOUSING TACTICS

In the realm of frugal living, your choice of living space can significantly impact your budget. Let's explore practical and thrifty strategies for managing housing expenses wisely.

1. Strategic Location, Strategic Savings: Evaluate the cost of commuting when choosing a location. Sometimes, a slightly higher rent in a closer location can be more economical when considering transportation expenses. Explore up-and-coming neighborhoods. These areas often provide a more affordable living option with the potential for increased property value over time.

Sarah works in the city but found a more affordable apartment in a suburb slightly farther away. She calculated potential commuting costs, factoring in public transportation or gas expenses. Sarah realized the lower rent offset the increased commuting costs, making the suburban option more economical.

2. Roommate Roulette - Shared Spaces for Shared Costs: Assess compatibility when choosing roommates. A harmonious living situation not only contributes to a pleasant environment but can also be financially beneficial. Clearly define responsibilities in the lease agreement. Ensure everyone understands their financial obligations to avoid potential conflicts.

James wanted to reduce rent expenses and decided to share a two-bedroom apartment with a friend. They discussed financial responsibilities, including rent, utilities, and shared costs like internet and groceries. By splitting living expenses, James and his friend were able to afford a better apartment than they could individually.

3. DIY Décor - Transforming Spaces on a Budget: Embrace thrifty DIY projects. Upcycling furniture or repurposing decor items can add a personal touch to your living space without breaking the bank. Participate in community exchange programs for home goods. These programs allow you to swap items with others, reducing the need for new purchases.

Emily wanted to personalize her apartment but couldn't afford expensive decor. She scoured thrift stores, repurposed old furniture, and even tried simple DIY projects like creating wall art from recycled materials. Emily achieved a unique, personalized living space without breaking the bank.

4. Utility Mastery - Efficient Living, Lower Bills: Invest in energy-efficient appliances. While the initial cost might be higher, the long-term savings on utility bills make it a frugal choice. Adopt water conservation practices. Simple habits like fixing leaks promptly and using water-saving devices can contribute to lower water bills.

Mark wanted to cut down on utility bills. He replaced old light bulbs with energy-efficient LED bulbs, fixed leaky faucets promptly, and adopted energy-saving habits like turning off appliances when not in use. Mark saw a noticeable reduction in his monthly utility bills.

5. Lease Negotiation Skills - Trimming Rental Costs: Negotiate flexible lease terms. Longer leases might offer lower monthly rent, while shorter leases provide more flexibility. Plan your move during off-peak seasons. Moving companies and landlords might be more willing to offer discounts during less busy times.

Alex wanted to negotiate a lower rent for his apartment. He researched average rental prices in the area, expressed his intention for a long-term lease, and politely discussed the possibility of a reduced rent. The landlord agreed to a slightly lower rent, acknowledging Alex's commitment to a longer lease.

6. Hidden Gems - Affordable Alternatives: Explore non-traditional housing options. Converted lofts, garage apartments, or even house-sitting arrangements can provide unique and cost-effective living spaces. Investigate community housing initiatives. Some communities offer affordable housing options with shared spaces, reducing individual costs.

Maria was looking for unique and affordable housing options. She explored converted lofts, finding a charming space with lower rent compared to traditional apartments. Maria discovered a distinctive living arrangement that not only suited her budget but also reflected her preference for unconventional spaces.

7. Digital Discounts - Online Real Estate Resources: Utilize specialized platforms for affordable housing. Some online resources focus on connecting individuals with reasonably priced rental options. Join local housing groups on social media. These groups often share information about affordable rentals and housing opportunities.

Jack needed to find an affordable place quickly. He joined local housing groups on social media, where he came across a reasonably priced rental posted by someone in his network. Jack secured a cost-effective living arrangement through his online connections.

8. Minimalist Living - Downsizing for Financial Freedom: Embrace mindful consumption. Assess your living space to determine what you truly need, allowing for downsizing and potential cost savings. Invest in efficient storage solutions. Clever organization can make a smaller living space feel more spacious and functional.

Rachel wanted to declutter her living space and save money. She assessed her possessions, donated items she no longer needed, and downsized to a smaller apartment. Rachel not only cut down on rent but also experienced the liberating benefits of a more minimalist lifestyle.

9. Community Living - Shared Facilities for Shared Savings: Explore co-housing concepts. Shared facilities, such as communal kitchens or laundry rooms, can significantly reduce individual living costs. Collaborate on maintenance tasks. Shared responsibilities for minor repairs and upkeep can save money collectively.

Jake sought cost-effective housing with shared amenities. He found a co-housing community with shared kitchens and communal spaces. Jake enjoyed reduced living expenses while fostering a sense of community with his co-residents.

10. Rent Negotiation Artistry - Advocating for Affordability: Conduct market research on rental prices in the area. Armed with this information, you can negotiate more effectively with landlords. Express your commitment to a long-term lease. Landlords may be more willing to negotiate if they believe you'll be a reliable tenant.

Olivia found a perfect apartment but felt the rent was slightly beyond her budget. Olivia respectfully negotiated with the landlord, citing comparable rental prices in the area and expressing her interest in a long-term lease. The landlord agreed to a moderate reduction, making the apartment more financially feasible for Olivia.

11. Creative Solutions - Live-Work Spaces: Negotiate remote work options with your employer. This opens up the possibility of living in more affordable areas without sacrificing career opportunities. Explore shared workspaces. These environments often provide cost-effective alternatives for professional work setups.

12. DIY Home Maintenance - Frugal Fixes: Invest time in learning basic home maintenance. Online tutorials and guides can empower you to tackle minor repairs without the need for professional assistance. Establish a tool-sharing network with neighbors. Sharing tools for occasional use reduces the need for every individual to invest in a full set.

13. Rent-to-Own Exploration - Gradual Ownership: Ensure clarity in rent-to-own agreements. Clearly defined terms and conditions protect both tenants and landlords in this unique arrangement. Use the rent-to-own period for financial planning. Save and invest wisely to ensure you're financially prepared when transitioning to ownership.

14. Government Housing Programs - Navigating Assistance: Research eligibility criteria for government housing programs. Many programs offer assistance to individuals or families with specific financial needs. Seek assistance with program applications. Non-profit organizations often provide support for navigating the application process.

15. Sustainable Living - Eco-Friendly and Economical: Explore renewable energy options. While upfront costs might be higher, long-term savings and environmental benefits make it an economically and ecologically sound choice. Participate in community gardening initiatives. Access to fresh produce can reduce grocery expenses while fostering a sense of community.

TAILORING TIPS TO DIVERSE CIRCUMSTANCES

- **Cultural Considerations:** Understand cultural influences on housing choices. Cultural norms can impact living preferences and the financial feasibility of certain options.

- **Economic Trends Awareness:** Stay informed about economic trends affecting the housing market. Adapting to evolving economic conditions ensures your housing choices remain financially prudent.

In navigating the landscape of economical living spaces, flexibility and creativity are key. Tailor these strategies to your unique circumstances, always considering your financial goals and lifestyle preferences.

PRACTICAL AND BUDGET-FRIENDLY DIY HOME SOLUTIONS

1. Pallet Furniture Magic - Crafty Recycling: You can find pallets for free in many places or get them at a low cost. Break them down, sand them, and you've got a versatile base for furniture. Add some paint, and you've created unique, environmentally friendly pieces. It is cost-effective and environmentally friendly. It allows customization to fit your space and style. Sarah transformed discarded pallets into a stylish and functional outdoor bench, saving on furniture costs.

2. Thrifty Textile Revamp - Funky Furniture Makeover: Thrift stores often have inexpensive fabric remnants. With a bit of creativity and a staple gun, you can transform your old furniture into something stylish and personalized. It refreshes the look of furniture without buying new. It personalizes your space with a touch of creativity. James revamped his worn-out couch by reupholstering it with a vibrant, inexpensive fabric, achieving a brand-new look.

3. DIY Wall Art - Your Art Gallery, Your Rules: Dive into DIY art with repurposed materials or simple painting techniques. Create a gallery wall with a mix of personal photos, paintings, and unique crafts. It's a reflection of your personality, and you don't need to spend much. It adds a personal touch to your home. It allows for artistic expression without high costs. Emily adorned her living room walls with a gallery of DIY art, making a statement on a shoestring budget.

4. Eco-Friendly Cleaning Solutions - DIY Clean Magic: Beyond saving money, making your cleaning solutions ensures you're using non-toxic ingredients. Vinegar, baking soda, and lemon not only clean effectively but also contribute to a healthier home environment. It saves money on commercial cleaning products. It reduces exposure to harmful chemicals. Mark concocted a DIY all-purpose cleaner that proved as effective as store-bought alternatives but at a fraction of the cost.

5. Budget-Friendly Flooring Makeover - Paint Magic: Painting your floor allows you to experiment with patterns, colors, and even faux finishes. It's an affordable way to refresh a room and express your creativity without the hefty price tag of new flooring. It provides a budget-friendly alternative to expensive flooring options. It allows for creativity in design and color choices. Alex revamped his outdated linoleum floor with a trendy painted pattern, achieving a stylish look without the hefty price tag.

6. Salvaged Salvos - Cool Vintage Touch: Scour salvage yards or online marketplaces for unique pieces with history. Incorporating salvaged items into your decor not only saves money but also adds character and a story to your home. It adds character to your space with unique, one-of-a-kind elements. It is often more affordable than buying new decorative pieces. Maria repurposed an antique door into a decorative tabletop, infusing her home with a touch of history.

7. Energy-Efficient Window Treatments - Cozy DIY Curtains: Sewing your thermal curtains allows you to customize them to fit your windows perfectly. Choosing energy-efficient materials can contribute to maintaining a comfortable temperature in your home, reducing the need for excessive heating or cooling. It reduces heating and cooling costs by improving insulation. It allows customization of curtain designs to match your decor. Jack crafted thermal curtains that not only enhanced the aesthetics of his home but also contributed to energy savings.

8. Upcycled Storage Solutions - Clever Storage Hacks: Upcycling items into storage solutions not only saves money but also encourages a sustainable lifestyle. It challenges you to think creatively about repurposing items that might otherwise end up in the landfill. It maximizes storage without investing in new furniture. It adds a touch of vintage charm to your home. Rachel repurposed an old wooden crate into a chic bookshelf, achieving both functionality and aesthetics.

9. Garden-Inspired Indoor Oasis - Easy Plant Life: Indoor gardening offers numerous benefits, from improved air quality to mental well-being. By starting with affordable plants and gradually expanding, you can create a thriving indoor garden that enhances your living space. It improves indoor air quality and adds a refreshing vibe. It is economical compared to buying pre-potted plants. Olivia propagated a few succulents from her existing collection, turning her living space into a thriving indoor garden.

10. Faucet Facelift - Kitchen Glow-Up on a Budget: Upgrading your kitchen faucet doesn't always require a new purchase. Sometimes, a simple change of handles or a fresh coat of paint can breathe new life into the existing fixture, saving you money while enhancing aesthetics. It enhances the look of the kitchen without a full-scale renovation. It is cost-effective compared to buying a new faucet. Jake replaced the handles on his kitchen faucet and spray-painted it, achieving a modern look without the expense of a new fixture

These deeper insights showcase the multifaceted advantages of incorporating these DIY solutions, from environmental consciousness to personal expression, all while keeping your budget intact. Dive in and make your home uniquely yours! These practical and economical DIY home solutions showcase how a bit of creativity and resourcefulness can lead to significant improvements without breaking the bank.

CHAPTER 5

PERSONAL NARRATIVES OF INDIVIDUALS WHO EMBARKED ON ECONOMICAL JOURNEYS, UNRAVELING THE INSIGHTS GAINED AND LESSONS LEARNED

MARIA'S DEBT-FREE JOURNEY - LIBERATION THROUGH FRUGALITY

Maria, a single mother of two, found herself drowning in the sea of debt. The burden was not just financial but also took a toll on her mental and emotional well-being. Faced with this crisis, Maria decided to take control by prioritizing frugality. She meticulously examined her spending habits, cut out unnecessary expenses, and embraced a minimalist lifestyle.

Maria's journey into frugality was not just about tightening her budget; it was a profound shift in perspective. She started distinguishing between needs and wants, discovering the joy that comes from living with less. By letting go of the constant pursuit of material possessions, Maria found a newfound sense of liberation. As she tackled each debt with determination, the weight lifted off her shoulders, and a sense of financial security began to replace the anxiety.

JOHN'S SUSTAINABLE LIVING ODYSSEY - FROM CONSUMERISM TO CONTENTMENT

John, a self-confessed shopaholic, had an epiphany about the environmental impact of his lifestyle. Motivated by a desire to reduce his carbon footprint, he embarked on a sustainable living journey. This involved not only cutting down on unnecessary purchases but also actively seeking out second-hand items, reducing waste, and even venturing into growing his own food.

John's story is more than just a shift in consumption patterns; it's a transformation in values. He discovered that true contentment doesn't come from accumulating possessions but from living in harmony with the planet. As he adopted eco-friendly practices, John not only contributed to environmental sustainability but also found a sense of purpose in his choices. His journey challenges the conventional notion of happiness tied to material abundance.

SARAH'S MINIMALIST LIFESTYLE - THRIVING WITH LESS

Sarah, seeking a change in her chaotic and cluttered life, embraced the principles of minimalism. Downsizing her living space, selling excess belongings, and adopting a "less is more" philosophy became the guiding principles of her journey.

Sarah's exploration of minimalism was a holistic endeavor. It wasn't just about decluttering her physical space but also decluttering her mind. By letting go of material excess, she created room for meaningful experiences and connections. The minimalist lifestyle became a source of joy, emphasizing quality over quantity. Sarah's story is a testament to the transformative power of simplifying life's complexities.

MARK'S DIY HOME PROJECT - BUDGET RENOVATION TRIUMPH

Faced with a tight budget for home renovations, Mark decided to take matters into his own hands. Armed with determination, online tutorials, and a frugal mindset, he ventured into a do-it-yourself (DIY) home improvement project.

Mark's journey goes beyond just fixing up his living space; it's about empowerment through skill acquisition. By learning to handle tasks himself, Mark not only saved a significant amount of money but also gained a newfound confidence. His story illustrates the potential for personal growth and financial savings that DIY projects offer. Mark's triumph is a reminder that with the right mindset, even seemingly daunting tasks can be tackled on a budget.

EMILY'S FINANCIAL TURNAROUND - FROM CRISIS TO CONTROL

Emily faced a financial crisis due to unexpected medical bills. Rather than succumbing to despair, she took proactive steps to regain control. This involved a meticulous reassessment of her spending, negotiations with creditors, and a focused approach to essential expenses.

Emily's journey is one of resilience and resourcefulness. In the face of adversity, she not only weathered the storm but emerged stronger. By building an emergency fund and exploring additional income streams, Emily turned a financial setback into an opportunity for growth. Her story is a testament to the transformative power of taking control of one's financial destiny, even in the most challenging circumstances.

JAMES AND LISA'S FAMILY BUDGETING - TEACHING KIDS THE VALUE OF MONEY

James and Lisa, recognizing the importance of financial education, involved their children in budgeting discussions. Together, they made collective decisions on spending priorities, fostering a sense of financial responsibility from a young age.

Their narrative extends beyond the realm of family finance; it's about instilling lasting values. James and Lisa's approach to financial education is proactive and inclusive. By involving their children in financial decisions, they not only teach budgeting skills but also cultivate a mindset of responsible money management. Their story is a blueprint for how families can work together to build a strong financial foundation for the future.

CHLOE'S SMALL BUSINESS SUCCESS - FRUGAL ENTREPRENEURSHIP

Chloe, fueled by passion and a shoestring budget, embarked on the entrepreneurial journey. Leveraging social media, networking, and embracing frugality, she turned her small business into a profitable venture.

Chloe's story is one of entrepreneurial resilience and creativity. In a world often dominated by financial barriers, she exemplifies that passion and resourcefulness can overcome budget constraints. Her journey underscores the possibilities that frugal entrepreneurship offers, where success is not solely measured by financial investment but by dedication and innovative thinking. Chloe's entrepreneurial triumph is an inspiration for those aspiring to turn their passions into sustainable ventures.

These personal narratives offer profound insights into the diverse ways individuals have embraced economical living. From debt liberation and sustainable choices to minimalist transformations and DIY victories, each story contributes to the rich tapestry of the economical lifestyle. Through challenges and triumphs, these narratives illuminate the transformative power of adopting an economical mindset, showcasing that the path to financial well-being is unique for each person.

CHAPTER 6

MASTERING CULINARY THRIFT: NAVIGATING THE WORLD OF BUDGET-FRIENDLY GASTRONOMY

Embarking on a journey of culinary thrift is akin to unlocking the secrets of creating delectable dishes while mindful of your budget. Let's delve into the art of smart cooking on a budget, exploring tactics that turn economical recipes into gastronomic delights while maximizing nutrition without a hefty price tag.

BUDGET-FRIENDLY COOKING TACTICS: CRAFTING CULINARY WONDERS WITHOUT BREAKING THE BANK

Example: Journey – Savvy Stir-Fry Soiree
Picture an evening where you transform basic, affordable ingredients into a culinary masterpiece. You opt for a vegetable stir-fry, making the most of discounted seasonal vegetables and a reasonably priced protein source such as tofu or chicken. This not only tantalizes your taste buds but also showcases the art of culinary thrift.

SMART COOKING TIPS

- **Harmony with the Seasons:** Align your recipes with seasonal produce. The vibrant freshness not only enhances flavor but is also budget-friendly.

- **Pantry Alchemy:** Choose pantry staples that play versatile roles. Ingredients like rice, lentils, and canned tomatoes can be culinary chameleons, offering budget-friendly adaptability.

- **Protein Prudence:** Explore protein sources that balance nutritional value with affordability. Legumes, eggs, and frozen seafood can be cost-effective culinary powerhouses.

- **Feeding Nutritional Abundance:** Maximizing Nutrition on a Budget.

- **Colorful Nutrient Palette:** Embrace a spectrum of colorful fruits and vegetables. This not only adds visual vibrancy to your plate but introduces a diverse range of essential nutrients.

- **Whole Grain Mastery:** Prioritize whole grains like quinoa and brown rice. They are not only budget-friendly but contribute to a more nutrient-dense meal.

- **Smart Fats Inclusion:** Incorporate budget-friendly, healthy fats like olive oil and avocado for both flavor and nutritional benefits.

DIFFERENT MEALS AND THEIR PREPARATION

Budget-friendly Pasta Bake: One-Pan Marvel
Ingredients:
- 2 cups of pasta (penne or any preferred type)
- 1 can (14 oz) of diced tomatoes
- Budget-friendly vegetables of your choice (bell peppers, zucchini and onions)
- 1 cup of shredded cheese (cheddar or mozzarella)
- Olive oil, salt, and pepper for seasoning

Preparation:
- Cook the pasta according to package instructions. Drain and set aside.
- In a pan, sauté the diced vegetables in olive oil until they are tender.
- Preheat your oven to 375°F (190°C).

- In a large mixing bowl, combine the cooked pasta, sautéed vegetables, diced tomatoes (with the juice), and half of the shredded cheese. Mix well.
- Transfer the mixture to a baking dish and sprinkle the remaining cheese on top.
- Bake in the preheated oven for about 20 minutes or until the cheese is melted and bubbly.
- Serve hot and enjoy your budget-friendly pasta bake!

Versatile Veggie Stir-Fry: Quick and Flavorful
Ingredients:

- Assorted seasonal vegetables (bell peppers, broccoli, carrots, snap peas)
- Protein of your choice (tofu, chicken, or shrimp)
- Soy sauce
- Sesame oil
- Garlic and ginger (minced)
- Cooked rice

Preparation:

- Cut the vegetables and protein into bite-sized pieces.
- In a wok or large pan, heat sesame oil over medium-high heat.

- Add minced garlic and ginger, stir-frying for about 30 seconds.
- Add the protein and cook until browned. Remove from the pan and set aside.
- In the same pan, stir-fry the vegetables until they are crisp-tender.
- Add the cooked protein back to the pan.
- Pour soy sauce over the mixture and stir well to combine.
- Serve the stir-fry over cooked rice.

Budget-Friendly Greens Smoothie: Nutrient-Packed Bliss

Ingredients:
- Handful of budget-friendly greens (spinach, kale)
- 1 cup frozen berries (strawberries, blueberries)
- 1/2 cup yogurt
- Water or milk for blending

Preparation:
- In a blender, combine the greens, frozen berries, and yogurt.
- Add water or milk based on your preferred consistency.
- Blend until smooth.
- Pour into a glass and enjoy your budget-friendly greens smoothie!

Economic Buddha Bowl: Nutritional Powerhouse
Ingredients:

- Cooked quinoa
- Budget-friendly vegetables (cucumbers, cherry tomatoes, avocados)
- Canned chickpeas (rinsed and drained)
- Olive oil and lemon juice for dressing

Preparation:

- Arrange cooked quinoa in a bowl.
- Add sliced vegetables and chickpeas on top.
- Drizzle with olive oil and lemon juice.
- Toss the ingredients together before enjoying your economic Buddha Bowl!

Economical Omelet Roll-Up: Morning Delight
Ingredients:

- 3 eggs
- Budget-friendly vegetables (bell peppers, onions, spinach)
- Cheese slices
- Salt, pepper, and a pinch of paprika for seasoning

Preparation:
- Whisk the eggs in a bowl and season with salt, pepper, and paprika.
- In a non-stick pan, sauté the diced vegetables until tender.
- Pour the whisked eggs over the vegetables, creating a thin layer.
- Place cheese slices on top and let it cook until the edges are set.
- Roll up the omelet and slice into bite-sized rolls.
- Serve hot for a quick and budget-friendly breakfast!

Frugal Chickpea Salad: Simple and Satisfying

Ingredients:
- Canned chickpeas (rinsed and drained)
- Cherry tomatoes, halved
- Cucumber, diced
- Red onion, finely chopped
- Feta cheese, crumbled
- Olive oil and balsamic vinegar for dressing

Preparation:
- In a bowl, combine chickpeas, cherry tomatoes, cucumber, red onion, and feta cheese.

- Drizzle olive oil and balsamic vinegar over the salad.
- Toss gently to coat all ingredients in the dressing.
- Chill in the refrigerator before serving your frugal chickpea salad.

Low-Cost Lentil Soup: Hearty and Healthy
Ingredients:
- Dry lentils
- Carrots, diced
- Celery, chopped
- Onions, finely chopped
- Garlic, minced
- Vegetable broth
- Cumin, coriander, and bay leaves for seasoning

Preparation:
- In a pot, sauté onions and garlic until fragrant.
- Add carrots and celery, cooking until they soften.
- Pour in vegetable broth, dry lentils, and season with cumin, coriander, and bay leaves.
- Simmer until lentils are tender, creating a hearty and low-cost lentil soup.

Affordable Banana Bread: Sweet Treat on a Budget

Ingredients:

- Ripe bananas, mashed
- Flour, sugar, and baking soda
- Eggs and butter
- Vanilla extract

Preparation:

- Mix mashed bananas, flour, sugar, baking soda, eggs, melted butter, and vanilla extract in a bowl.
- Pour the batter into a greased loaf pan.
- Bake until a toothpick inserted comes out clean, delivering a delightful and affordable banana bread.

These recipes showcase that delicious and nutritious meals don't have to strain your budget. By incorporating simple, wholesome ingredients, you can create a variety of satisfying dishes without compromising on taste or health. 🍌🍎🍞

MAXIMIZING NUTRITION ON A BUDGET: SMART TIPS

1. Buy in Bulk: Purchase non-perishable items like grains, legumes, and spices in bulk. This often comes at a lower unit price, saving you money in the long run.

2. Embrace Frozen Produce: Frozen fruits and vegetables are not only budget-friendly but also retain their nutritional value. They are versatile and can be used in various recipes.

3. Plan Your Meals: Create a weekly meal plan based on budget-friendly ingredients. This helps prevent impulse purchases and ensures you use ingredients efficiently.

4. Explore Generic Brands: Opt for store-brand or generic products, which are often more affordable than their branded counterparts. The quality is often comparable, providing savings without sacrificing taste.

5. DIY Snacks and Staples: Make your snacks and pantry staples at home. Examples include granola bars, yogurt, and salad dressings. This allows you to control ingredients and save money.

6. Use Leftovers Wisely: Repurpose leftovers into new meals. For instance, last night's roasted vegetables can become a filling for a budget-friendly omelet or a topping for a grain bowl.

7. Shop Seasonal Produce: Focus on buying fruits and vegetables that are in-season. They tend to be more abundant and, therefore, less expensive.

8. Explore Affordable Proteins: Incorporate budget-friendly protein sources such as beans, lentils, and canned tuna into your meals. These alternatives are not only economical but also rich in nutrients.

9. Cook in Batches: Prepare meals in large batches and freeze portions for later. This prevents food waste and provides convenient, ready-to-eat options when time is limited.

10. DIY Herb Garden: Grow your herbs at home. A small herb garden on your windowsill can save money on buying fresh herbs regularly.

Last month, I decided to challenge myself to create budget-friendly yet nutritious meals for the entire week. One of my favorites was the versatile veggie stir-fry. Not only did it allow me to use up leftover vegetables in the fridge, but the combination of colors and flavors made it a delightful and nutritious option. Plus, cooking in batches meant I had tasty lunches for days, eliminating the need for pricey takeout. This experience taught me the importance of strategic planning and the incredible variety of budget-friendly meals that can be whipped up with a little creativity.

By incorporating these tips and recipes into your routine, you not only save money on groceries but also promote a healthier lifestyle.

SMART GROCERY CART CHRONICLES: NAVIGATING THE AISLES LIKE AN ECONOMIST

Welcome to the advanced level of mastering the art of grocery shopping with an economist's finesse.

Let's delve into each strategy, unlocking the secrets to not just saving, but thriving within your budget.

- **Strategic Planning Before the Expedition:** The backbone of economical grocery shopping is a well-thought-out shopping list. Take the time to plan your meals for the week, considering what's on sale and what you already have at home. This meticulous planning minimizes impulsive purchases, ensuring that you only buy what you need.

  As I planned my meals in advance, I not only saved money but also cut down on food waste, utilizing ingredients across multiple dishes.

- **Embracing the Art of Comparison:** The aisles are a battlefield of choices, and arming yourself with the skill of comparison is crucial. Don't settle for the first item you see; instead, scrutinize different brands and sizes. You'll be surprised how a simple shift in brand or quantity can lead to significant savings. Through consistent comparison, I discovered that certain generic brands offered equal quality at a fraction of the cost of premium alternatives.

- **The Dance of Discounts:** Discounts and promotions are your best allies in the grocery shopping adventure. Keep an eye on the store's circular, app notifications, or even dedicated discount sections. These opportunities are not just about saving money; they often introduce you to new products. Taking advantage of a two-for-one deal on canned goods not only saved me money but also introduced me to a brand I now regularly include in my pantry.

- **Navigating the Perimeter:** The perimeter of the store is a goldmine for fresh, budget-friendly options. It's where you find fruits, vegetables, meats, and dairy – the essentials of a balanced and economical diet. Opting for fresh produce over pre-packaged snacks not only improved the nutritional quality of my meals but also aligned with my budget goals.

- **Decoding Unit Prices:** Consider unit prices as your secret decoder ring in the grocery world. They allow you to cut through marketing tactics and truly understand the cost of a product per unit. It's a small effort that pays off in substantial savings. Calculating unit prices made me realize that sometimes, buying in bulk is not always the most cost-effective option, especially for perishable items.

- **Flexibility in Brand Loyalty:** Loyalty is commendable, but sometimes, a little flexibility can go a long way. Experiment with different brands and store labels; you might discover hidden gems that not only satisfy your taste buds but also align with your budget goals. Trying a store-brand version of my preferred cereal turned out to be a win-win – delicious and economical.

- **Loyalty Programs and Rewards:** Don't underestimate the power of loyalty programs. Sign up for your local grocery store's program, and reap the benefits of discounts, exclusive offers, and accumulated points. It's a symbiotic relationship where both you and the store win. Loyalty programs not only saved me money at the checkout but also provided opportunities for additional perks like free products or special promotions.

So, armed with these advanced strategies, step into the grocery store like an economist on a mission. Your cart is not just a vessel for groceries; it's a tool for financial empowerment. Happy shopping! 🛒🍐🛍️

CHAPTER 7

NAVIGATING THE SHOPPING MAZE: CRAFTY TIPS FOR ECONOMICAL WINS

Embark on a shopping journey enriched with nuanced strategies that not only save you money but elevate your shopping prowess to an art form.

These practical tips go beyond the basics, offering insightful ways to identify value and avoid unnecessary expenses.

MASTERING THE ART OF LIST MAKING - CRAFTING YOUR SHOPPING BLUEPRINT

Crafting a list isn't just about jotting down items; it's about sculpting a blueprint for your shopping adventure. Dive deeper by categorizing your list based on priority, ensuring that essentials take precedence. Creating a detailed list not only helped me stay focused but also allowed me to streamline my purchases based on immediate needs and long-term goals.

TIMING IS EVERYTHING - THE SYMPHONY OF SHOPPING SEASONS

Understanding the rhythm of sales cycles and discount days requires a deeper dive into retail patterns. Delve into research on seasonal clearances and exclusive promotions, orchestrating your purchases for maximum savings. Unearthing the intricate dance of retail timing turned my shopping into a strategic symphony, with each purchase hitting the right note of savings.

EMBRACE THE POWER OF COUPONS - FROM CLIPPING TO DIGITAL MASTERY

Coupons are more than pieces of paper; they are potent tools in the savvy shopper's arsenal. Dive deeper by exploring digital couponing platforms and understanding the art of stacking coupons for compounded savings. Venturing beyond traditional couponing methods revealed a world of digital discounts and exclusive offers, significantly enhancing my cost-cutting strategies.

QUALITY OVER QUANTITY - THE ART OF DISCERNING VALUE

Crafty shopping transcends mere frugality; it's about discerning value. Dive deeper into product research, understanding the lifespan of items, and recognizing the distinction between cost-effective and cheap. Prioritizing quality transformed my mindset. It's not just about spending less; it's about investing wisely to reduce the frequency of replacements.

BEFRIEND THE CLEARANCE SECTION - TREASURES IN THE UNEXPLORED

The clearance section isn't just a corner; it's a realm of hidden treasures. Delve deeper by frequenting this area, understanding the store's clearance patterns, and recognizing the art of finding high-value items at unbeatable prices.

Navigating the clearance section became an adventure, unveiling items I hadn't considered and leading to substantial savings on premium products.

QUESTION EVERY PURCHASE - MINDFUL SHOPPING AS A LIFESTYLE

The art of questioning isn't a one-time endeavor; it's a lifestyle. Dive deeper into the psychology of your purchases, understanding the impact of each buy on your budget and long-term financial goals. Cultivating a habit of questioning every purchase became a mindfulness practice, aligning my spending habits with my values and priorities.

DIGITAL PRICE MATCHING - THE TECH-INFUSED SHOPPING STRATEGY

The smart phone isn't just a device; it's your ally in price matching. Delve deeper by exploring price-matching apps, understanding retailers' policies, and mastering the art of securing the best deal in real-time. Incorporating digital price matching into my routine not only saved me money but empowered me with the confidence that I was getting the best possible price.

MINDFUL ONLINE SHOPPING - NAVIGATING THE VIRTUAL MARKETPLACE

Online shopping is more than a convenience; it's a realm of opportunities. Dive deeper into the world of online promotions, exclusive discounts, and the art of navigating virtual platforms for maximum savings. Online shopping became a strategic endeavor, allowing me to explore a plethora of options, compare prices effortlessly, and access deals not available in brick-and-mortar stores.

In the intricate tapestry of crafty shopping, every decision is an opportunity for financial mastery. Delve into these strategies not just as tips but as elements that contribute to a holistic approach, transforming your shopping experience into a strategic and empowering journey. Happy crafting!

CHAPTER 8

PASSING ON ECONOMIC WISDOM - TEACHING THE NEXT GENERATION (INSTILLING ECONOMIC HABITS IN CHILDREN)

LEAD BY EXAMPLE: THE SILENT TEACHER

Parents often underestimate the impact of their actions on children. By showcasing frugal habits, like comparing prices or opting for homemade snacks, parents become silent but influential teachers. Children absorb these behaviors and values naturally, forming a foundation for responsible financial habits in the future.

When I faced a choice between buying snacks or making them at home, I consciously chose the latter. My child, observing this, began to appreciate the effort and cost-effectiveness of homemade treats.

FINANCIAL LITERACY THROUGH PLAY: GAMES THAT EDUCATE

Learning is most effective when it's enjoyable. Introducing children to board games or digital apps that simulate financial scenarios transforms complex concepts into engaging activities. These games foster a sense of curiosity and understanding about money management. Our family game nights became an opportunity to play "Budget Builders." Not only did it teach financial concepts, but it also turned learning into a fun and interactive experience.

INCENTIVIZE SAVING: TURNING HABITS INTO REWARDS

Children respond well to incentives. By associating saving money with tangible rewards, such as a special treat or outing, kids learn that financial responsibility comes with its own set of positive outcomes. Our family introduced a "Savings Jar" where a portion of the weekly allowance went. When it accumulated to a certain amount, we used it for a family outing. This practice encouraged consistent saving.

OPEN CONVERSATIONS ABOUT MONEY: BREAKING THE TABOO

Creating an open environment for discussing money is crucial. Children need to understand that finances are a regular part of life, and open conversations help demystify the topic. This approach builds trust and encourages children to ask questions. During our monthly budget discussions, we involve our child. This openness has led to insightful discussions about needs versus wants and the importance of planning.

SETTING AND ACHIEVING FINANCIAL GOALS: A FAMILY AFFAIR

Goal-setting instills purpose and responsibility. By involving the whole family in setting achievable financial goals, children learn the value of teamwork and collective efforts to achieve desired outcomes. Planning a weekend getaway became a family goal. We discussed how saving collectively could make it happen, teaching our child about setting priorities and working together towards a common objective.

INTRODUCING THE CONCEPT OF EARNING: CHORES FOR COMPENSATION

Understanding the relationship between work and earnings is a fundamental lesson. By linking specific chores to monetary rewards, children grasp the concept of earning, instilling a sense of responsibility and a connection between effort and financial gain. Our child takes on extra chores for a small reward. This practice teaches the importance of effort, responsibility, and the concept of earning in a tangible and relatable way.

CHAPTER 9

HANDY ECONOMIC STRATEGIES - DIVERSE THRIFT TECHNIQUES (ASSORTED ECONOMIC TIPS)

BUDGET-FRIENDLY GROCERY SHOPPING HACKS: MAXIMIZING SAVINGS IN THE AISLES

Grocery shopping can be a strategic affair. Beyond basic tips, delve into more advanced strategies such as understanding sales cycles, using cash back apps, and leveraging loyalty programs. The goal is not just to save money but to maximize value for every dollar spent. By strategically timing our grocery shopping to coincide with sales and using cash back apps, we not only saved money but also earned rewards that further contributed to our budget.

TRANSPORTATION THRIFT - FROM COMMUTES TO ROAD TRIPS

Transportation costs extend beyond the fuel pump. Dive deeper into economical strategies such as carpooling, maintaining a fuel-efficient driving style, and exploring budget-friendly road trip options. These strategies not only save money but also contribute to environmental sustainability. Carpooling with colleagues not only reduced individual commuting costs but also fostered a sense of community among co-workers.

TECH-SAVVY SAVING - APPS AND PLATFORMS FOR FINANCIAL GAINS

The digital landscape offers numerous opportunities for financial management. Explore a variety of apps and platforms that not only assist in budgeting but also provide insights into spending patterns and potential areas for savings. Using budgeting apps helped us identify patterns in discretionary spending and set realistic goals for saving. The real-time updates created awareness and encouraged mindful spending.

DIY HOME MAINTENANCE - THRIFTY SOLUTIONS FOR A WELL-KEPT HOME

Home maintenance can be a significant expense, but it doesn't have to be. Delve into practical do-it-yourself solutions for common household issues, from fixing leaks to basic repairs. These skills not only save money on professional services but also empower homeowners. Learning to fix minor plumbing issues and perform routine maintenance tasks has not only saved us money but also provided a sense of accomplishment and self-sufficiency.

STRATEGIC SUBSCRIPTION MANAGEMENT - EVALUATING AND OPTIMIZING

Subscriptions often accumulate unnoticed. A closer look at various subscriptions, from streaming services to magazines, can unveil opportunities for consolidation and optimization. This process not only saves money but also declutters life from unnecessary expenses. Reevaluating our subscriptions revealed that we were paying for services we rarely used. Consolidating and canceling unnecessary subscriptions freed up funds for more meaningful experiences.

CHAPTER 10

GROWING SAVINGS IN YOUR GARDEN - ECONOMICAL GARDENING WISDOM (TIPS FOR BUDGET-FRIENDLY GARDENING)

SEED STARTING AND PROPAGATION: COST-EFFECTIVE GARDEN BEGINNINGS

The journey of a garden begins with seeds. Explore the art of seed starting and propagation, turning a single seed packet into multiple plants. This not only reduces the need for purchasing established plants but also adds a personalized touch to the gardening process. Starting plants from seeds allowed us to experiment with a variety of flowers and vegetables without breaking the bank. It also became a rewarding aspect of our gardening journey.

COMPOSTING - NUTRIENT-RICH SOIL ON A BUDGET

Soil enrichment is key to a thriving garden. Delve into the world of composting, transforming kitchen scraps and yard waste into nutrient-rich soil amendments. This not only reduces the need for store-bought fertilizers but also contributes to sustainable gardening practices. Implementing composting reduce our reliance on commercial fertilizers. The nutrient-rich compost not only improved soil quality but also minimized waste.

RAINWATER HARVESTING - FREE WATER FOR YOUR GARDEN

Watering can contribute significantly to your gardening costs. Explore the simple and cost-effective technique of rainwater harvesting for your garden. Installing a rain barrel in our backyard not only reduced our water bills but also ensured our plants received natural, unchlorinated water.

VERTICAL GARDENING - MAXIMIZING SPACE AND YIELD

Limited space doesn't mean limited produce. Delve into the concept of vertical gardening, optimizing space and increasing your garden yield. Growing herbs and small vegetables vertically on our balcony railing allowed us to enjoy fresh produce without needing a large garden plot.

DIY GARDEN STRUCTURES - FRUGAL SOLUTIONS FOR PLANT SUPPORT

Garden structures can be expensive, but they don't have to be. Explore do-it-yourself solutions for plant support, creating sturdy structures without a hefty price tag.

Constructing simple trellises from repurposed materials not only provided support for climbing plants but also added a rustic charm to our garden.

CHAPTER 11

BUDGET-FRIENDLY CELEBRATIONS - CELEBRATING ON A DIME (PLANNING BUDGET-FRIENDLY EVENTS)

DIY DECORATIONS: CRAFTING AMBIANCE WITHOUT BREAKING THE BANK

Decorations contribute to the festive atmosphere but can be costly. Delve into do-it-yourself decoration ideas, adding a personal touch to your celebrations. Creating paper decorations for a birthday party not only saved money but also allowed us to tailor the theme to the individual's preferences.

POTLUCK PARTIES - SHARING THE JOY AND THE MEAL

Hosting a meal for a gathering can strain your budget. Explore the concept of potluck parties, where everyone contributes a dish, making the celebration a shared effort. Organizing a potluck Thanksgiving dinner not only eased the burden on the host but also ensured a diverse and delicious meal.

THEMED CELEBRATIONS ON A BUDGET - CREATIVITY OVER COST

Themed parties can be memorable without being extravagant. Delve into the art of planning themed celebrations on a budget, focusing on creativity rather than cost. Hosting a movie night with a DIY home theater and homemade snacks turned out to be a hit with friends without a hefty price tag.

DIGITAL INVITATIONS - ECO-FRIENDLY AND COST-EFFECTIVE

Invitations can be elegant without the need for paper and postage. Explore the world of digital invitations, saving both money and the environment. Creating digital invitations for a graduation party not only saved printing costs but also allowed for easy RSVP tracking.

DIY GIFTS -THOUGHTFUL GESTURES OVER PRICEY PRESENTS

Gifts can be meaningful without being expensive. Delve into the realm of do-it-yourself gifts, adding a personal touch to your celebrations. Handmade photo albums for special occasions not only showcased cherished memories but also conveyed thoughtfulness and care.

Celebrating on a dime is not about compromising on joy but about maximizing the warmth and significance of the moment. These budget-friendly celebration ideas are a testament to the creativity and resourcefulness that can elevate any event without straining your finances. 🎉💰🏠

CONCLUSION

In conclusion, "The Ultimate Guide to an Economical Living" not only serves as a beacon for financial empowerment but also as a companion on the transformative journey towards a more purposeful and economically conscious life.

Authored by the insightful and experienced Amber G. Sallee, this guidebook transcends traditional financial advice, offering a unique blend of relatable anecdotes, savvy economic insights, and actionable strategies.

Readers are taken on a comprehensive exploration, from mastering budgeting basics to delving into the world of thrifty culinary adventures, all presented with simplicity, depth, and a human touch. The book provides a roadmap for seamlessly integrating economic principles into daily routines, ensuring that financial well-being becomes a tangible and achievable goal.

"The Ultimate Guide to an Economical Living" goes beyond the realm of financial management; it becomes a guide to holistic living. Whether you're a parent seeking balance, an aspiring entrepreneur navigating the business world, or anyone aiming to enhance economic resilience, Amber's guide offers invaluable tools for reshaping your financial narrative.

As the final chapter unfolds, readers are left with a sense of empowerment, armed with the knowledge and inspiration needed to embark on a journey towards financial freedom. Amber G. Sallee's book is not just a guide; it's a companion that encourages readers to embrace a brighter financial future and live life on their terms.

With every turn of the page, "The Ultimate Guide to an Economical Living" invites you to take control of your financial destiny and savor the joy of living economically.

I HAVE A REQUEST

Dear Reader,

I hope this message finds you well. I'm reaching out because your feedback is incredibly important to us, especially as someone who has engaged with "The Ultimate Guide to an Economical Living."

We value your thoughts and insights on how the book has impacted your understanding of economical living and financial empowerment. Your review will not only help us refine our future offerings but will also contribute to the community seeking practical and relatable guidance.

Whether you found the book insightful, transformative, or have suggestions for improvement, we want to hear from you. Your honest review will be instrumental in shaping the experience for others who embark on their journey toward financial well-being.

We appreciate you taking the time to share your perspective.

Thank you for your support!

Warm regards,

AMBER G. SALLEE

Author.

www.ingramcontent.com/pod-product-compliance
Lightning Source LLC
Chambersburg PA
CBHW060103260726
48658CB00004B/1384